# HEROIC COMPANION DOGS

Written by Annabel Griffin

Illustrated by Marina Halak

Copyright © 2024 Hungry Tomato Ltd

First published in 2024 by Hungry Tomato Ltd
F15, Old Bakery Studios, Blewetts Wharf, Malpas Road, Truro, Cornwall,
TR1 1QH, UK.

No part of this publication may be reproduced, stored in a retrieval system, or transmitted in any form or by any means, electronic, mechanical, photocopying, recording, or otherwise, without prior written permission of the copyright owner.

A CIP catalogue record for this book is available from the British Library.

ISBN 9781916598720

Printed in China

Discover more at
www.hungrytomato.com

# CONTENTS

| | |
|---|---|
| The World of Dogs | 4 |
| Breed Groups | 6 |
| Heroic Companions | 8 |
| Pocket-size pups | 9 |
| Mini Versions | 14 |
| Heroic Helpers | 16 |
| Popular Pooches | 20 |
| Crossbreeds | 22 |
| What's That Dog? | 24 |
| Spot the Dog | 26 |
| Caring For Your Pup | 28 |
| Glossary | 30 |
| Index | 31 |

Words in **BOLD** can be found in the glossary.

# THE WORLD OF DOGS

**Get ready to explore the wonderful world of heroic companions! From the tiny toy dogs to the amazing therapy dogs, there are so many different types of lovable dogs to discover.**

Wolf or dog? Who knows.

## WHERE DO DOGS COME FROM?

Believe it or not, all dogs are **descendants** of ancient wolves. The details of how and when wolves became dogs are still quite foggy, but it likely started when humans began to **domesticate** and train wolves, at least 14,000 years ago. Today, dogs can be found all over the world.

Pug or Beagle?

## WHAT IS A CROSSBREED?

A **crossbreed** is a dog whose parents are from two or more different breeds. Some crosses are well-loved, as they can combine the best bits from their parent breeds. Crossbreeds and mongrels are also often less likely to have health problems than **purebreds**. You can find some popular crossbreeds on pages 22-23.

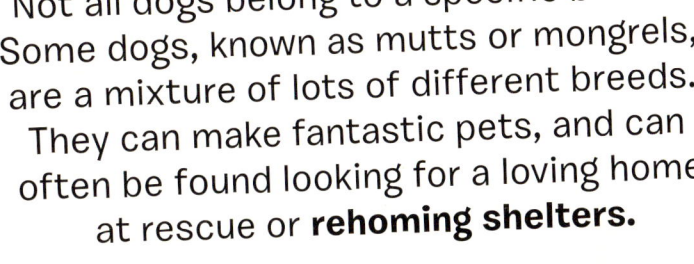

## WHAT IS A BREED?

A breed is a particular group of dogs that all share the same (or very similar) appearance and **characteristics**, making them easy to identify. There are hundreds of different breeds, and they can vary wildly in size, shape, hairiness, and personality.

Not all dogs belong to a specific breed. Some dogs, known as mutts or mongrels, are a mixture of lots of different breeds. They can make fantastic pets, and can often be found looking for a loving home at rescue or **rehoming shelters.**

*Big and small, they've got it all!*

## GETTING A DOG?

Maybe you already have a dog in your family, or maybe you'd like to in the future. Owning a dog can be fun and rewarding, but it's also a big responsibility. Some dogs need a lot of space, time and attention. Before buying or **adopting** a dog, you should always carefully research their breed and think about whether you are able to give them everything they need to be happy.

*Look how cute and cuddly they are!*

# BREED GROUPS

Dog breeds are often arranged into seven different groups, that are loosely based on the jobs that they were originally bred to do.

## SPORTING GROUP

Also known as gundogs, these dogs were originally bred to help hunters retrieve birds.

## NON-SPORTING GROUP

This is the group for dogs that don't fit into any of the other groups, so they are quite a mixed bunch!

## TERRIER GROUP

This group were originally bred to hunt burrowing animals, such as rats, rabbits, foxes, and badgers. Most of them have "terrier" as part of their name.

## WORKING GROUP

Dogs in this group were originally bred to perform practical tasks, such as pulling sleds and carts. They were also often used as watchdogs. They are usually large dogs.

**SIGHTHOUNDS**
These dogs are usually long, lean and very fast.

**SCENT HOUNDS**
These dogs have droopy ears and powerful noses.

# HOUND GROUP

Hounds were bred for their sense of smell or sight, and were usually used for hunting. They can be split into two sub-groups: sighthounds and scent hounds.

# HERDING GROUP

This group includes dogs that were bred to work on farms; herding and guarding livestock, such as sheep and cows.

# TOY GROUP

Tiny breeds that are small enough to sit in your lap fall into this group. They are bred mostly as pets and companions.

# HEROIC COMPANIONS

It is often said that dogs are "mankind's best friend". They can be loving, loyal and funny companions. Some dogs are even able to provide emotional and physical support to people who need them. From fluffy little lapdogs to supportive **service dogs**, the dogs in this book all make fantastic human companions.

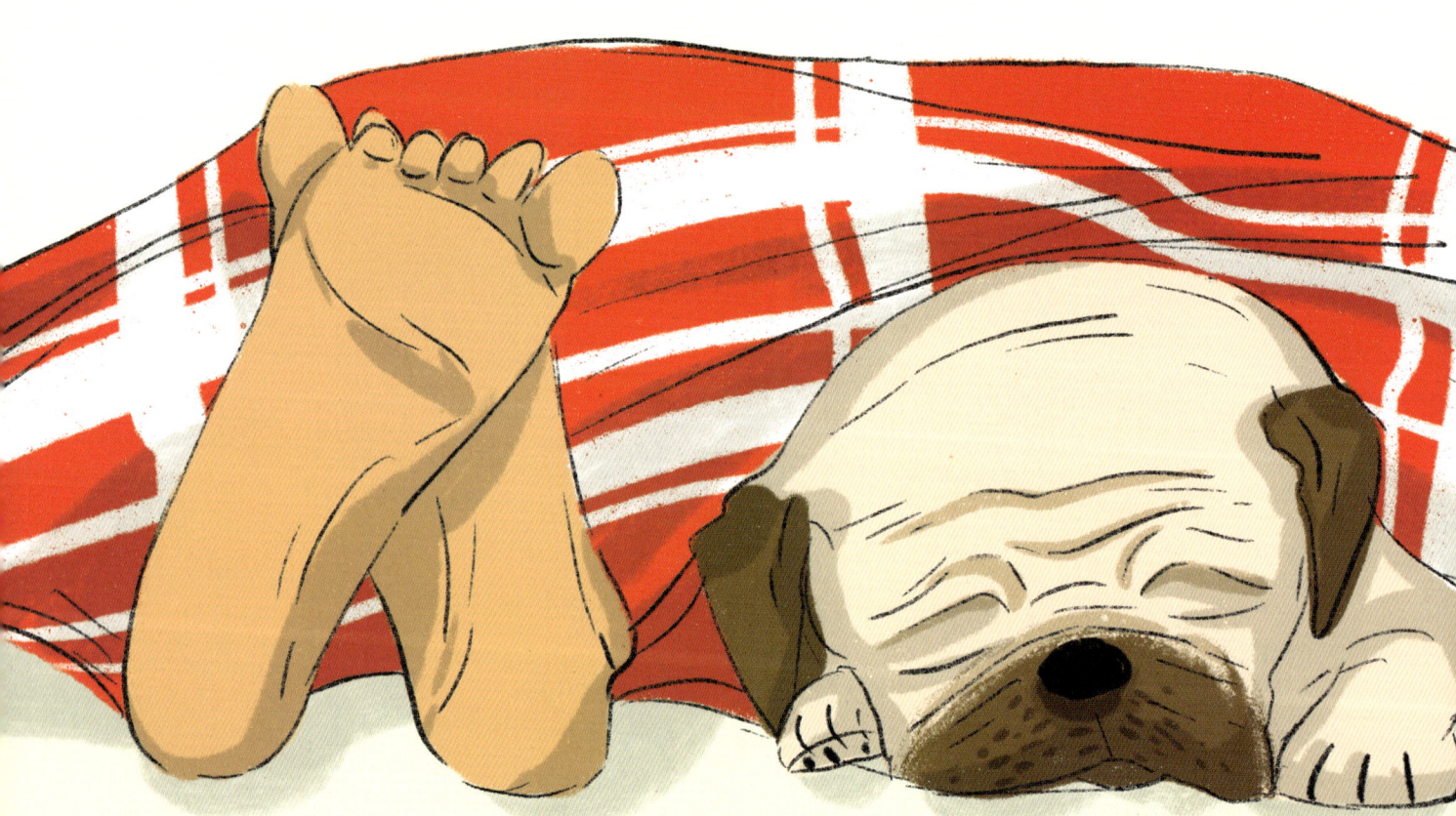

# POCKET-SIZE PUPS    9

# Pug

These popular pups have a long history as **lapdogs**. They were the valued companions of ancient Chinese emperors, and became popular among wealthy Europeans, from the 16th century. Their squished faces often lead to difficulty breathing, and other health problems.

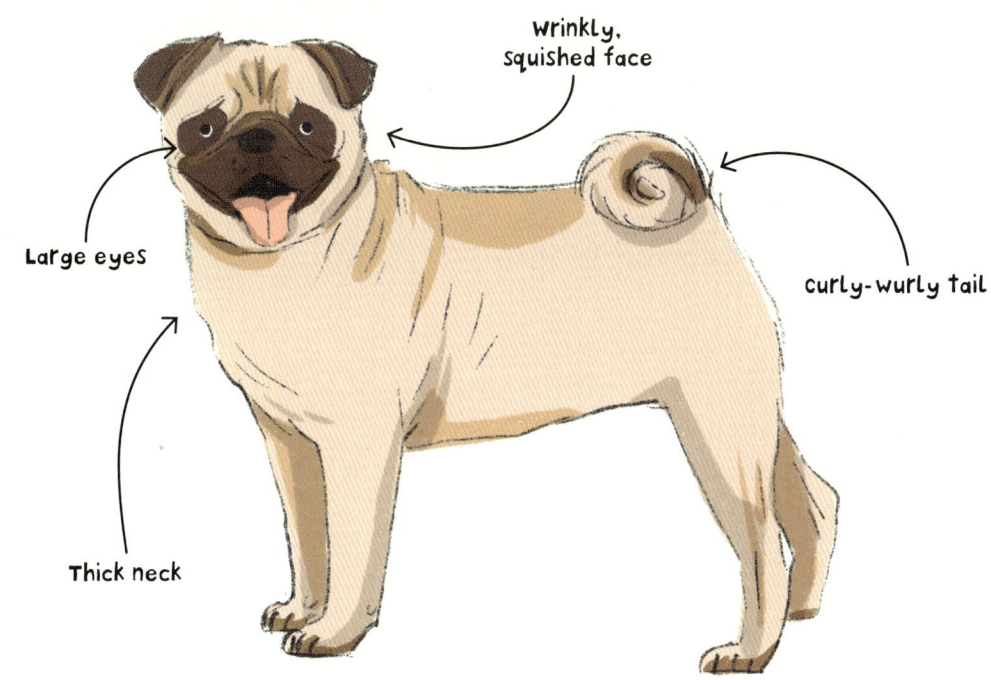

wrinkly, squished face

Large eyes

curly-wurly tail

Thick neck

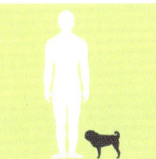

**ORIGIN:** China

**COAT:** Short, smooth

**PERSONALITY:** Loving and mischievous

INTELLIGENCE

ENERGY LEVEL

TRAINABILITY

# 10 POCKET-SIZE PUPS

## Papillon

This tiny breed can be easily identified by its large, feathery ears. Papillons appear on the laps of royalty in many old European paintings. They are affectionate dogs who love to play.

Large butterfly wing ears (Papillon means "butterfly" in French)

Long, plumed tail

Small, pointed muzzle

**ORIGIN:** France/Belgium
**COAT:** Medium-length, silky
**PERSONALITY:** Clever and friendly

INTELLIGENCE
ENERGY LEVEL
TRAINABILITY

## Boston Terrier

This smart-looking little dog is nicknamed "the American Gentleman". They make good pets for people who live in towns and cities. They are playful and love people.

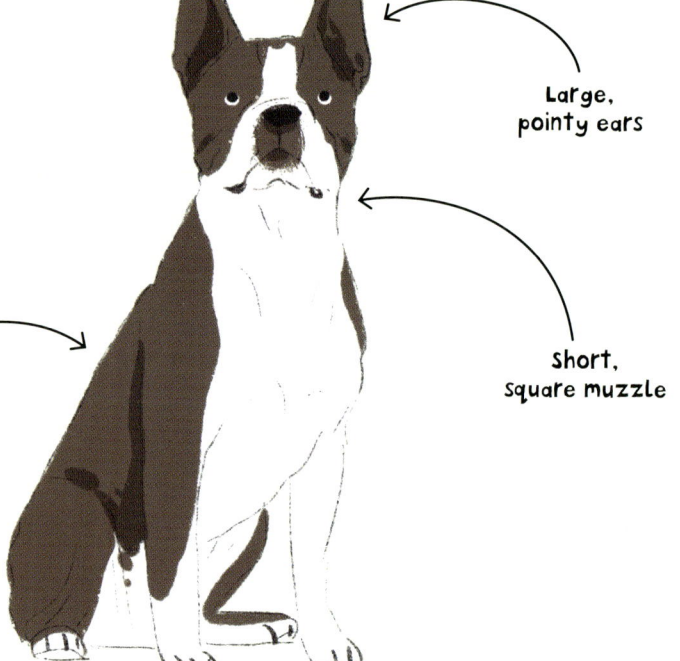

Large, pointy ears

Short, square muzzle

Black and white tuxedo-like coat

**ORIGIN:** USA
**COAT:** Short, smooth
**PERSONALITY:** Funny and outgoing

INTELLIGENCE
ENERGY LEVEL
TRAINABILITY

POCKET-SIZE PUPS    11

# Brussels Griffon (Griffon Bruxellois)

This unusual toy breed (see page 7) has a big personality for its size! They are playful and easy to train. They love to be part of the family and can get lonely when left on their own for too long.

- Bearded face
- Short muzzle
- can also have short, smooth coats

**ORIGIN:** Belgium
**COAT:** Medium-length, **wiry**
**PERSONALITY:** Loyal and playful

INTELLIGENCE 🐾🐾🐾🐾🐾
ENERGY LEVEL 🐾🐾🐾🐾🐾
TRAINABILITY 🐾🐾🐾🐾🐾

# Cavalier King Charles Spaniel

These dogs are named after King Charles II of England, who kept similar dogs. Unlike most other breeds of spaniel, who were originally bred to work, these dogs have always been kept purely for companionship.

- Long, fluffy ears
- Silky coat
- Feathery legs

**ORIGIN:** United Kingdom
**COAT:** Medium-length, wavy, silky
**PERSONALITY:** Gentle and affectionate

INTELLIGENCE 🐾🐾🐾🐾🐾
ENERGY LEVEL 🐾🐾🐾🐾🐾
TRAINABILITY 🐾🐾🐾🐾🐾

# POCKET-SIZE PUPS

## French Bulldog

This mini bulldog breed is a popular pet. They are particularly good for people who live in small houses or flats, as they don't need a lot of outdoor exercise. They also make handy watchdogs, as they are always alert.

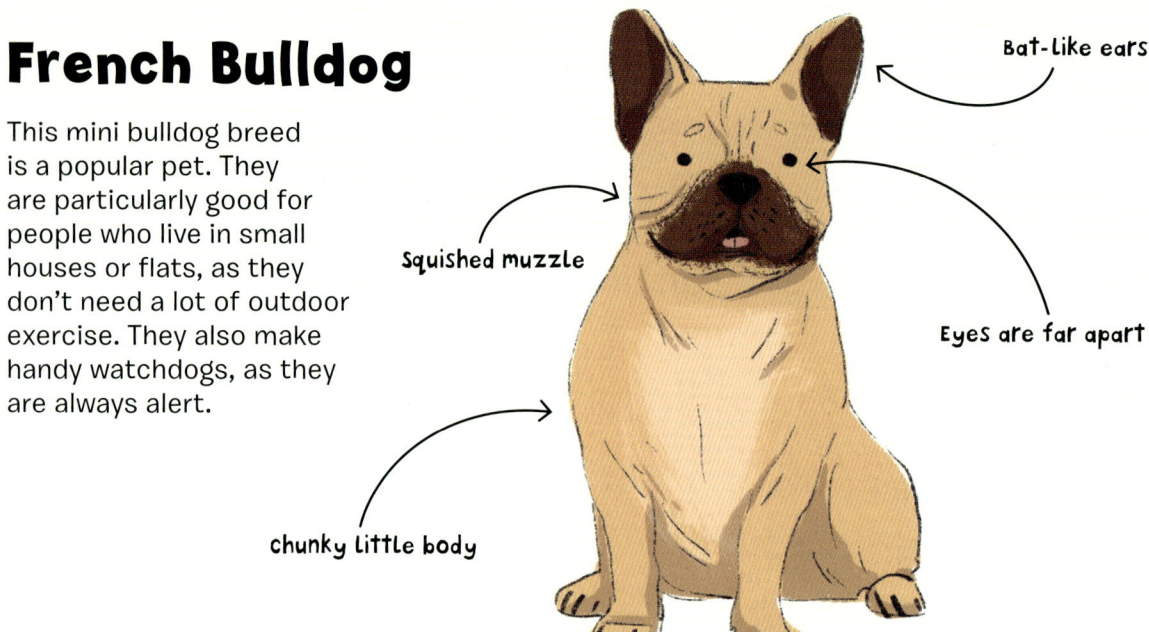

- Bat-like ears
- Squished muzzle
- Eyes are far apart
- chunky little body

**ORIGIN:** France
**COAT:** Short, smooth
**PERSONALITY:** Goofy and charming

**INTELLIGENCE:** 🐾🐾🐾
**ENERGY LEVEL:** 🐾🐾🐾
**TRAINABILITY:** 🐾🐾🐾🐾

## Shih Tzu

The Mandarin name "Shih Tzu" translates to "little lion" in English. Their long, fluffy coats require a lot of grooming, but they make cuddly and playful pets.

- Floppy ears (somewhere under all the fluff)
- Short muzzle
- Fluffy tail
- Some owners clip their coats to a shorter "teddy bear" cut

**ORIGIN:** China/Tibet
**COAT:** Long, thick
**PERSONALITY:** Playful and affectionate

**INTELLIGENCE:** 🐾🐾
**ENERGY LEVEL:** 🐾🐾🐾🐾
**TRAINABILITY:** 🐾🐾🐾🐾🐾

POCKET-SIZE PUPS 13

# Bolognese

These scruffy little dogs are real couch potatoes that don't require a lot of exercise. They love being with people and don't like to be left alone for long.

- Black button nose
- Needs a lot of grooming
- Non-shedding, fluffy coat

**ORIGIN:** Italy
**COAT:** Long, wavy
**PERSONALITY:** Calm and easy-going

INTELLIGENCE 🐾🐾🐾🐾🐾
ENERGY LEVEL 🐾🐾
TRAINABILITY 🐾🐾🐾🐾🐾

# Japanese Chin

Despite their name, these dogs are thought to have first originated in China. They are often described as cat-like dogs, and make excellent lap-warmers!

- Big, wide-set, boggly eyes
- Sheds a lot of hair!
- Fluffy tail curves over back
- Short muzzle

**ORIGIN:** China
**COAT:** Medium-length, silky
**PERSONALITY:** Gentle and loving

INTELLIGENCE 🐾🐾🐾
ENERGY LEVEL 🐾🐾🐾
TRAINABILITY 🐾🐾🐾

# 14 MINI VERSIONS

## Toy Poodle

The smallest of four different sizes of the popular poodle, reaching a maximum of 25cm tall. They may be tiny, but they are just as smart and athletic as their larger brothers and sisters.

Thick, curly coat

Can be clipped and groomed in different styles

Weighing under 2.7kg

**ORIGIN:** Germany
**COAT:** Long, curly
**PERSONALITY:** Smart and confident

INTELLIGENCE: 🐾🐾🐾🐾🐾
ENERGY LEVEL: 🐾🐾🐾🐾
TRAINABILITY: 🐾🐾🐾🐾🐾

## Miniature Pinscher

Also known as "Min Pins", these dogs are a mini breed of pinscher that look similar to the larger German pinscher and Dobermann. They were originally used as farmyard rat-hunters.

Straight back

Upright tail

Shiny, black and tan coat

**ORIGIN:** Germany
**COAT:** Short, smooth
**PERSONALITY:** Fearless and outgoing

INTELLIGENCE: 🐾🐾🐾🐾
ENERGY LEVEL: 🐾🐾🐾🐾🐾
TRAINABILITY: 🐾🐾🐾

MINI VERSIONS 15

# Alaskan Klee Kai

This miniature husky-type dog comes in three sizes, with a height range between 30-44cm. They look similar to the much larger Siberian husky and Alaskan malamute, but were bred as house dogs, rather than to pull sleds.

Large, pointy ears

Loosely curled tail

Thick coat

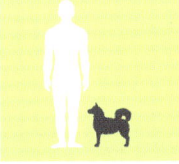

**ORIGIN:** USA
**COAT:** Medium-length, extra thick
**PERSONALITY:** Alert and curious

INTELLIGENCE
ENERGY LEVEL
TRAINABILITY

# Shetland Sheepdog

The Shetland sheepdog, or "Sheltie", is often mistaken for a mini rough collie, but they are actually separate breeds. They are one of the smartest dogs around and are incredibly loving, but they need lots of exercise and attention.

Lion-like mane

Long, thick coat needs a lot of grooming

Fluffy tail

**ORIGIN:** United Kingdom
**COAT:** Long, very thick
**PERSONALITY:** Loyal and sensitive

INTELLIGENCE
ENERGY LEVEL
TRAINABILITY

# HEROIC HELPERS

Service or assistance dogs are trained to help people with disabilities. This includes guide dogs for the blind and visually impaired, hearing dogs to assist deaf and hard of hearing people, mobility service dogs to help people with physical disabilities, and medical response dogs to help people manage medical conditions.

A service dog's duties can include helping people move around, completing household tasks, providing medical assistance, and offering emotional support and company. Lots of different breeds are used as service dogs, but some are particularly popular.

Guide dog for the blind

# HEROIC HELPERS

## Labrador Retriever

Labs have long been the most popular dog in many countries around the world. They are loving, highly intelligent, steady and reliable. These are all great qualities for guide dogs for the blind, and for other service and assistance work.

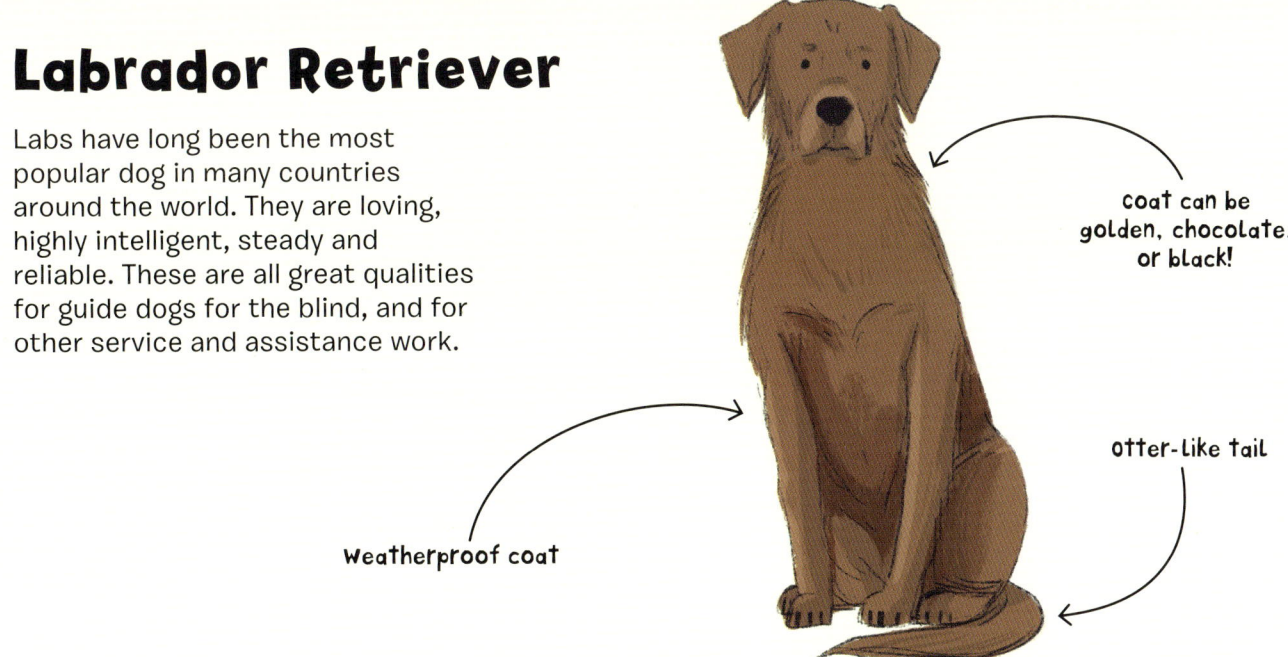

coat can be golden, chocolate, or black!

otter-like tail

Weatherproof coat

**ORIGIN:** Canada
**COAT:** Short, smooth
**PERSONALITY:** Lovable and loyal

INTELLIGENCE
ENERGY LEVEL
TRAINABILITY

Wide head

# HEROIC HELPERS

## Golden Retriever

Another very popular breed, as both family pets and for service work. Golden retrievers are big people-pleasers which makes them affectionate family pets and also clever working dogs.

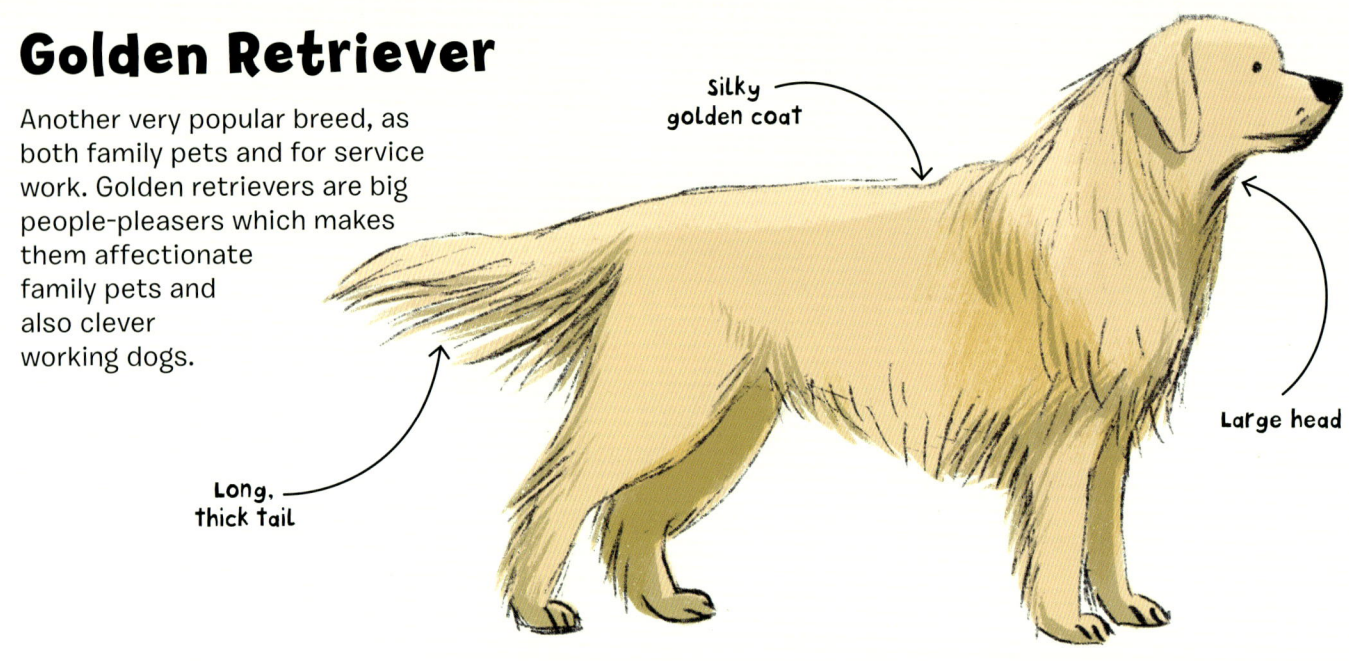

- Silky golden coat
- Large head
- Long, thick tail

**ORIGIN:** United Kingdom
**COAT:** Medium-length, thick
**PERSONALITY:** Gentle and trustworthy

INTELLIGENCE
ENERGY LEVEL
TRAINABILITY

They can be easily trained to perform many different tasks, including laundry!

HEROIC HELPERS 19

# Irish Setter

Often known simply as "red setters" because of their distinctive auburn coat. Their sweet, affectionate and sociable personalities have made them popular as **therapy dogs**, to be taken into schools, hospitals and nursing homes.

Loving eyes

Long, silky ears

Glossy red coat

**ORIGIN:** Ireland
**COAT:** Medium-length, silky
**PERSONALITY:** Lovable and loyal

INTELLIGENCE 🐾 🐾 🐾 🐾 🐾
ENERGY LEVEL 🐾 🐾 🐾 🐾 🐾
TRAINABILITY 🐾 🐾 🐾 🐾 🐾

# Pomeranian

Service dogs don't have to be big! Aside from being adorable balls of fluff, Pomeranians are highly intelligent and loving. They make great emotional support dogs, medical response dogs, and can also assist people who have difficulties hearing or have no hearing at all.

Fluffy coat

Super soft and fluffy

Foxy face

**ORIGIN:** Germany
**COAT:** Long, very thick
**PERSONALITY:** Friendly and clever

INTELLIGENCE 🐾 🐾 🐾 🐾 🐾
ENERGY LEVEL 🐾 🐾 🐾 🐾 🐾
TRAINABILITY 🐾 🐾 🐾 🐾 🐾

# POPULAR POOCHES

## Shiba Inu

This ancient breed has been much loved in its homeland of Japan for centuries, and has recently been gaining popularity across the rest of the world.

- Pointy ears
- Smiley face
- Cat-like personality

**ORIGIN:** Japan
**COAT:** Short, thick
**PERSONALITY:** Bold and independant

INTELLIGENCE: 🐾🐾🐾
ENERGY LEVEL: 🐾🐾🐾
TRAINABILITY: 🐾🐾

## English Cocker Spaniel

One of the most popular spaniel breeds, English cocker spaniels are energetic, alert, and loyal. They can make fun and affectionate pets for active families.

- Loving eyes
- Long, floppy ears
- Feathery legs and belly

**ORIGIN:** United Kingdom
**COAT:** Medium-length/long, wavy
**PERSONALITY:** Friendly and outgoing

INTELLIGENCE: 🐾🐾🐾🐾🐾
ENERGY LEVEL: 🐾🐾🐾🐾
TRAINABILITY: 🐾🐾🐾🐾

POPULAR POOCHES 21

# Staffordshire Bull Terrier

"Staffies" often have a bad **reputation** because of their history as fighting dogs, but they are actually some of the sweetest, most affectionate dogs you will ever meet!

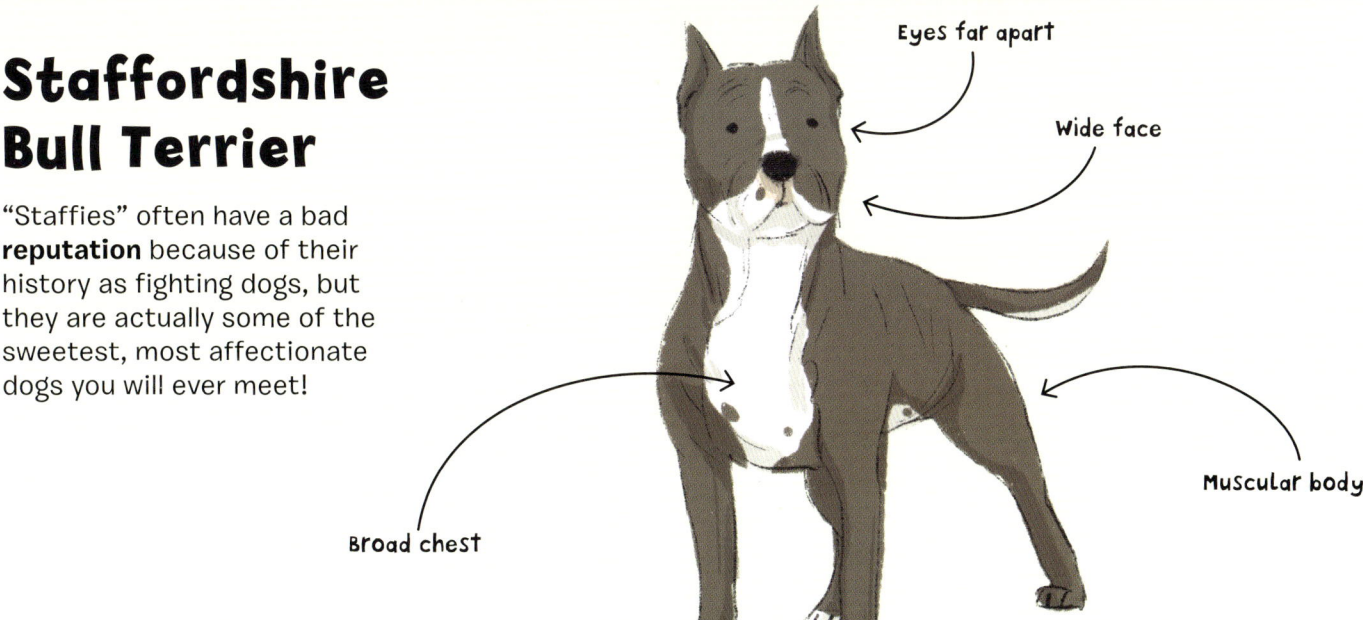

Eyes far apart
Wide face
Muscular body
Broad chest

| | |
|---|---|
| ORIGIN: United Kingdom | INTELLIGENCE 🐾🐾🐾 |
| COAT: Short, smooth | ENERGY LEVEL 🐾🐾🐾🐾 |
| PERSONALITY: Brave and loyal | TRAINABILITY 🐾🐾🐾🐾 |

# Shar-Pei

This unusual-looking breed is thought to have developed from ancient Chinese guard dogs. They came near to **extinction** in the 1970s, but are now a popular breed across the world. Unfortunately, irresponsible breeding for a more wrinkled look has increased their risk of health problems.

Small, floppy ears

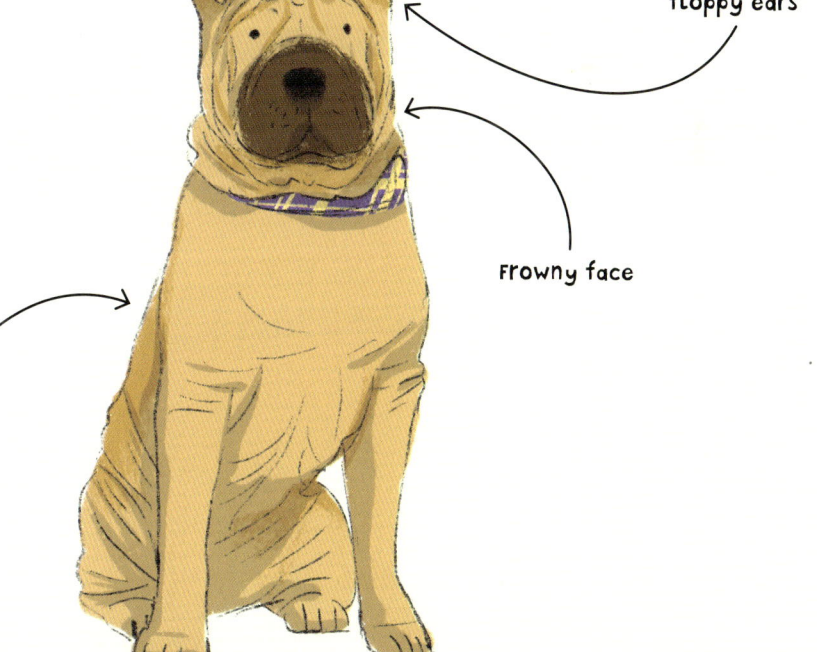

Frowny face

Wrinkly skin

| | |
|---|---|
| ORIGIN: China | INTELLIGENCE 🐾🐾🐾 |
| COAT: Short, smooth | ENERGY LEVEL 🐾🐾🐾 |
| PERSONALITY: Lovable and loyal | TRAINABILITY 🐾🐾 |

# CROSSBREEDS

## Labradoodle

Labradoodles are a cross between a Labrador retriever (page 17) and a poodle. They have become incredibly popular family dogs. They are smart, energetic, and people-loving.

- Floppy ears
- Usually have a curly coat
- Size can vary

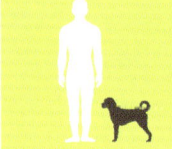

**ORIGIN:** Australia
**COAT:** Medium-length, curly
**PERSONALITY:** Playful and friendly

INTELLIGENCE
ENERGY LEVEL
TRAINABILITY

## Lurcher

Lurchers are a cross between a sighthound (see page 7), such as a greyhound or whippet, and a terrier or herding dog. They are usually gentle and quiet dogs who love to run, but spend lots of their time relaxing and snoozing, too.

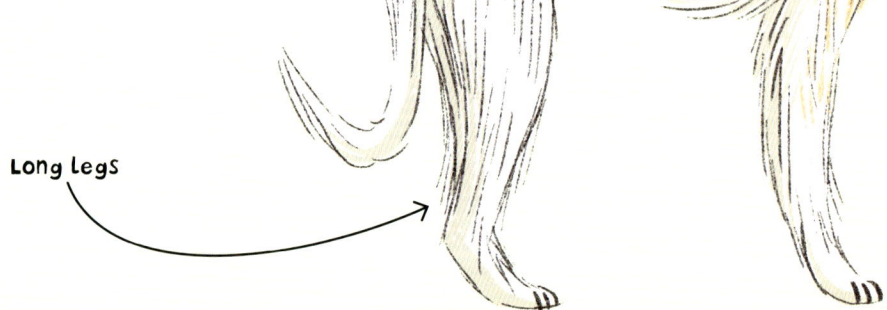

- Athletic body
- Long, pointy nose
- Appearance and size varies depending on which breeds have been crossed
- Long legs

**ORIGIN:** United Kingdom
**COAT:** Short, smooth or wiry
**PERSONALITY:** Peaceful and loving

INTELLIGENCE
ENERGY LEVEL
TRAINABILITY

CROSSBREEDS 23

# Puggle

A puggle is a cross between a pug (page 9) and a beagle. They are taller and more energetic than a pug, and are less likely to have health issues.

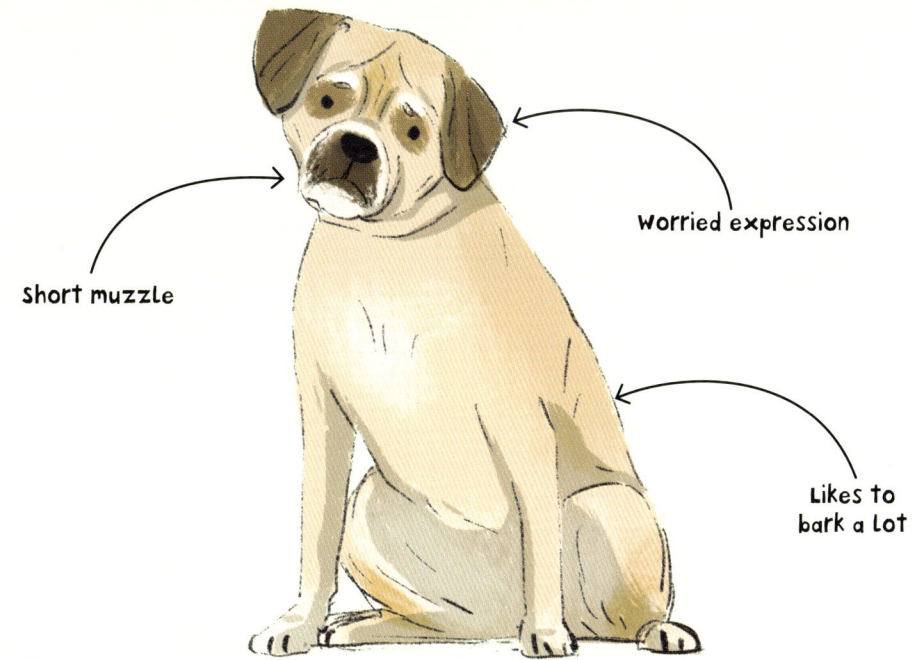

Short muzzle
Worried expression
Likes to bark a lot

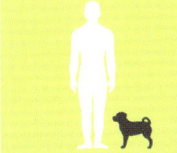

**ORIGIN:** USA
**COAT:** Short, smooth
**PERSONALITY:** Bouncy and outgoing

INTELLIGENCE
ENERGY LEVEL
TRAINABILITY

# Cavachon

This cute little pup is a cross between a Cavalier King Charles spaniel (page 11) and a bichon frisé. They can make fun-loving, loyal companions.

Short, floppy ears
Fluffy coat
Teddy bear or dog?

**ORIGIN:** USA
**COAT:** Medium-length, wavy or curly
**PERSONALITY:** Cuddly and playful

INTELLIGENCE
ENERGY LEVEL
TRAINABILITY

# WHAT'S THAT DOG?

Now that you have read all about heroic companion dogs, how good are you at identifying them? There are 25 different dogs to figure out. Use the information in the book to help you.

**1**

**What am I?**
A. Shiba Inu
B. Lurcher
C. Labradoodle

**2**

**What am I?**
A. Cavachon
B. Alaskan Klee Kai
C. Shar Pei

**3**

**What am I?**
A. Puggle
B. Papillon
C. Shih Tzu

**4**

**What am I?**
A. Labrador Retriever
B. Irish Setter
C. Shiba Inu

**5**

**What am I?**
A. Boston Terrier
B. Shetland Sheepdog
C. Irish Setter

**6**

**What am I?**
A. Cavachon
B. Pug
C. Bolognese

**7**

**What am I?**
A. Japanese Chin
B. Shar Pei
C. Miniature Pinscher

**8**

**What am I?**
A. Toy Poodle
B. Pomeranian
C. Japanese Chin

**9**

**What am I?**
A. Cavalier King Charles Spaniel
B. Bolognese
C. Staffordshire Bull Terrier

**10**

**What am I?**
A. English Cocker Spaniel
B. Golden Retriever
C. Boston Terrier

**11**

**What am I?**
A. Pug
B. Brussels Griffon
C. Papillon

**12**

**What am I?**
A. Staffordshire Bull Terrier
B. Shar Pei
C. Miniature Pinscher

25

**What am I?**
A. Shiba Inu
B. Puggle
C. Irish Setter

Answers can be found on page 32.

**What am I?**
A. Japanese Chin
B. Boston Terrier
C. Lurcher

**What am I?**
A. Toy Poodle
B. Cavachon
C. English Cocker Spaniel

**What am I?**
A. Alaskan Klee Kai
B. French Bulldog
C. Golden Retriever

**What am I?**
A. Pomeranian
B. Staffordshire Bull Terrier
C. Labradoodle

**What am I?**
A. Shih Tzu
B. Labradoodle
C. French Bulldog

**What am I?**
A. Bolognese
B. Labrador Retriever
C. Pomeranian

**What am I?**
A. Miniature Pinscher
B. Papillon
C. Brussels Griffon

**What am I?**
A. Puggle
B. Shar Pei
C. Golden Retriever

**What am I?**
A. French Bulldog
B. Toy Poodle
C. Shetland Sheepdog

**What am I?**
A. Golden Retriever
B. Pug
C. Cavalier King Charles Spaniel

**What am I?**
A. Lurcher
B. English Cocker Spaniel
C. Shetland Sheepdog

**What am I?**
A. Shih Tzu
B. Brussels Griffon
C. Alaskan Klee Kai

# SPOT THE DOG

There are so many brilliant dogs in the world. You can see them everywhere you go: in towns, parks, and sometimes even at the beach! See which of these are the most popular dogs where you live, make a note of them in a notebook if you do spot them.

**Brussels Griffon**  **Shiba Inu**  **Shar-Pei**
**French Bulldog**  **Alaskan Klee Kai**  **Pomeranian**

Which dogs do you think will be the most and least common in your area? Write your guesses in a notebook and check if you were right. You may be suprised how many you spot, now that you know your breeds!

Pug

Toy Poodle

Staffordshire Bull Terrier

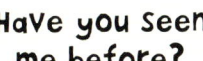
Shih Tzu

English Cocker Spaniel

Golden Retriever

Have you spotted me when you're out-and-about?

Have you seen me before?

Cavachon

Labradoodle

Puggle

Lurcher

Labrador Retriever

Shetland Sheepdog

# CARING FOR YOUR PUP

Owning a dog can be fun and rewarding, but it's also a big responsibility. There are lots of things to think about when looking after your four-legged friend.

## Grooming

Just like people, dogs need to have their hair (fur), nails and teeth looked after regularly. You can do basic grooming at home and take your pup to a professional groomer when they need a haircut!

Brush your pup's coat every day to stop it from tangling.

Regular baths are advised, and after a muddy walk... essential!

Dogs need their teeth cleaned too! Clean them with dog-safe toothpaste or a special chew toy.

Dogs that don't walk on hard surfaces need to have their nails clipped.

# Exercise

All dogs need daily exercise. Whether you're walking around your neighbourhood or playing in the dog park, your dog will love getting out and exercising. It's fun and keeps them healthy!

Some dogs, like Shetland Sheepdogs, have lots of energy and need 1-2 long walks a day.

Other dogs, like Bologneses, only need one short walk a day.

# Health

It's important to make sure your dog is healthy, so pay attention if they start behaving differently to normal. Signs of illness could include:

- Limping or holding a paw off the ground
- Heavy panting for no reason
- Change to eating or drinking habits

Speak to an adult if you think something's wrong, they can take the pup to a **vet**. Vets can also provide the de-worming and flea medicines dogs need regularly to stay healthy.

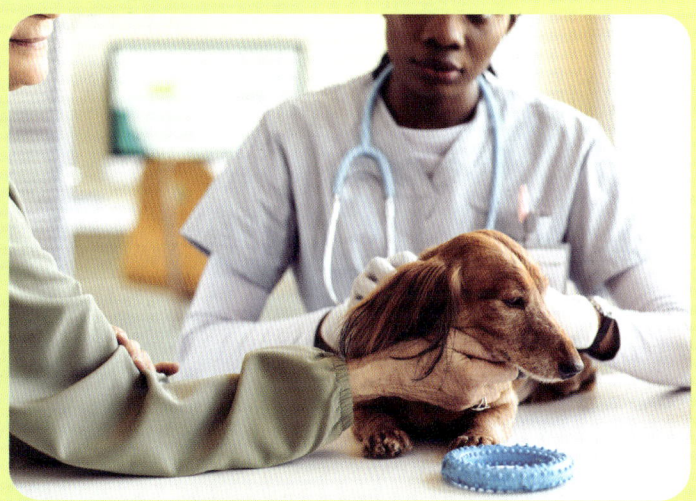

# Diet

There are lots of options for dog food, including dry biscuits and tinned food. The amount your dog needs to eat every day depends on their age, size and breed. Giving them the right amount is important for keeping them healthy and happy.

Be careful if you use treats for training, you don't want to overfeed your pup!

# GLOSSARY

**Adopting** – Legally taking on the animal as your own, receiving all responsibility.

**Characteristics** – a feature or quality of a person, place, or thing.

**Crossbreeding (crossbreeds)** – when two dogs of different breeds have puppies.

**Descendants** – people or animals that are related to an individual or group who lived in the past. For example, you are a descendant of your parents and grandparents.

**Domesticate** – to be tamed or trained to live or work with humans.

**Extinction** – the dying out of a species.

**Lapdogs** – dogs that are small enough to sit on someone's lap and make friendly companions.

**Purebreds** – dogs belonging to a specific breed, not a crossbreed or mongrel.

**Rehoming shelter** – a place where dogs (or other animals) who were lost, stray, or given up by their owners, are looked after until they can be adopted into a new home.

**Reputation** – A general opinion based on beliefs about a certain thing or person.

**Service dog (or assistance dog)** – a dog that has been trained to assist a person with a disability. Examples of service dogs include guide dogs, hearing dogs, medical response dogs, and autism service dogs.

**Therapy dog** – dogs that are trained to provide comfort and support to people. Unlike service dogs (see above) who only assist one person, therapy dogs help multiple individuals, or groups of people. They often work in hospitals, schools, or nursing and retirement homes.

**Vet** - a vet, or veterinarian, is an animal doctor. They help take care of animals when they are sick or hurt.

**Wiry** – a type of dog coat that is rough, thick, and bristly.

# INDEX

**A**
Alaskan klee kai 15, 26
Alaskan malamute 15

**B**
bichon frisé 23
beagle 23
Bolognese 13, 29
Boston terrier 10
Brussels griffon (Griffon Bruxellois) 11, 26

**C**
cavachon 23, 27
Cavalier King Charles spaniel 11, 23
crossbreeds 4, 22-23, 30

**D**
Dobermann 14

**E**
English cocker spaniel 20, 27

**F**
French bulldog 12, 26

**G**
German pinscher 14
golden retriever 18, 27
greyhound 22

**H**
herding group 7, 22
hound breed group 7

**I**
Irish setter 19

**J**
Japanese Chin 13

**L**
labradoodle 22, 27
Labrador retriever 17, 22, 27
lurcher 22, 27

**M**
miniature pinscher 14

**N**
non-sporting breed group 6

**P**
papillon 10
Pomeranian 19, 26
poodle 14, 22
pug 9, 23, 27
puggle 23, 27

**S**
scent hound 7
service dogs 8, 16-17, 18-19, 30
Shar-pei 21, 26
Shetland sheepdog 15, 27, 29
shiba inu 20, 26
shih tzu 12, 27
Siberian husky 15
sighthound 7, 22
sporting breed group 6
Staffordshire bull terrier 21, 27

**T**
terrier 6, 10, 21, 22, 27
therapy dogs 19, 30
toy breed 7, 11
toy poodle 14, 27

**W**
whippet 22

## WHAT'S THAT DOG ANSWERS

1 - B. Lurcher
2 - A. Cavachon
3 - C. Shih Tzu
4 - A. Labrador Retriever
5 - C. Irish Setter
6 - C. Bolognese
7 - B. Shar-Pei
8 - C. Japanese Chin
9 - A. Cavalier King Charles Spaniel
10 - A. English Cocker Spaniel
11 - B. Brussels Griffon
12 - C. Miniature Pinscher
13 - A. Shiba Inu
14 - B. Boston Terrier
15 - A. Toy Poodle
16 - C. Golden Retriever
17 - B. Staffordshire Bull Terrier
18 - B. Labradoodle
19 - C. Pomeranian
20 - B. Papillon
21 - A. Puggle
22 - A. French Bulldog
23 - B. Pug
24 - C. Shetland Sheepdog
25 - C. Alaskan Klee Kai

## ABOUT THE AUTHOR

Annabel is a writer and artist based in London, UK. Having worked as a bookseller for many years, she now writes children's books focusing on animals and the natural world. Her recent titles include *What Can I See in the Wild?*, *Seasons* and *The Spectacular Lives of Sharks*.

## ABOUT THE ILLUSTRATOR

Marina is a talented illustrator of children's books from Ukraine. Her stunning illustrations are inspired by her own childhood, children, nature, magical moments and fairytales.

Picture Credits:
(abbreviations: t=top, b=bottom, m=middle, l=left, r=right)

220 selfmade studio 25bm, 27tl; Anna Maloverjan 25mr; BIGANDT.COM 24bl; Chaoss 24tm, 27ml; Danita Delimont 25tm, 27tm; David Raihelgauz 24m, 26tr; Dezy 25ml, 27m; Dmytro Zinkevych 28ml; DragoNika 24ml; Ezzolo 29bl; Joy Brown 24tm, 27ml; Jus-01 28br; Kasefoto 28mr; Labrador photo video 24bm, 27m; Lisjatina 25bm, 27br; Littlekidmoment 28bl; Mary swift 25bl, 25mr, 26ml, 27mr; Meirion Matthias 24tl, 27bl; Momick 25br, 26m; Monkey Business Images 29mr; Nikola Cedikova 25tr, 27tr; OleysaNickolaeva 25t, 26tm; Otsphoto 24bm, 26tl; Priadilshchikova Natalia 24mr; Rala 303 25tm, 27mr; Rebeccaashworthearle 25tl; Roman Zaiets 25ml, 26mr; Rosa Joy 24tr, 27bm; SasaStock 24m; Serova_Ekaterina 24br.

Every effort has been made to trace the copyright holders, and we apologise in advance for any unintentional omissions. We would be pleased to insert the appropriate acknowledgements in any subsequent edition of this publication.